W9-AYI-647

HAMMERHEAD SHARKS

THE SHARK DISCOVERY LIBRARY

Sarah Palmer

Illustrated by Ernest Nicol and Libby Turner

Rourke Enterprises, Inc.
Vero Beach, Florida 32964

Library of Congress Cataloging-in-Publication Data

Palmer, Sarah, 1955-
    Hammerhead Sharks/Sarah Palmer; illustrated by Ernest
Nicol and Libby Turner

        p. cm. - (Sharks discovery library)
    Includes index.
    Summary: Describes the appearance, habitat, and
behavior of the three main kinds of hammerhead sharks.
    ISBN 0-86592-461-9
    1. Hammerhead sharks—Juvenile literature.
[1. Hammerhead Shark. 2. Sharks]   I. Nicol, Ernest, ill.
II. Title. III. Series: Palmer, Sarah,   1955-
Sharks discovery library.
QL638.95.S7P35   1989   88-4610
597'.31 - dc19   CIP
                               AC

TABLE OF CONTENTS

HAMMERHEAD SHARKS

Five **species** of hammerhead sharks are found in the oceans around the United States. The three most common kinds are the Great Hammerhead, the Scalloped Hammerhead, and the Smalleye Hammerhead. All hammerhead sharks are very strange looking. Their heads are flattened and shaped like hammers. This is how they got their name.

A Great Hammerhead shark

HOW THEY LOOK

Hammerhead sharks range in size from an average of 11 feet, for the female Great Hammerhead, to 4 feet, for the Smalleye Hammerhead. The Great Hammerhead and the Scalloped Hammerhead are greenish brown, and the Smalleye Hammerhead is gray. They all have white undersides. The largest known hammerhead was a Great Hammerhead measuring over 18 feet, 7 inches.

From top to bottom: Smalleye, Great and Scalloped Hammerhead sharks

WHERE THEY LIVE

The Scalloped Hammerhead is the most common of the five species and is found in warm waters all over the world. The Great Hammerhead lives mostly in shallow **reefs**, although it is sometimes seen in quite deep waters. The little Smalleye Hammerhead stays in inshore waters, close to land. It has been known to live in fresh water rivers.

*Great Hammerheads live mostly
in shallow lagoons*

WHAT THEY EAT

All hammerhead sharks eat bony fish, squid, crabs, and sometimes smaller sharks. The Great Hammerheads' favorite food is the stingray. Great Hammerheads are often found with the barbs from stingrays' tails in and around their mouths. One had as many as fifty stuck in his mouth. The Smalleye Hammerhead is known to eat baby Scalloped Hammerheads.

Smalleye Hammerheads sometimes eat baby Scalloped Hammerheads

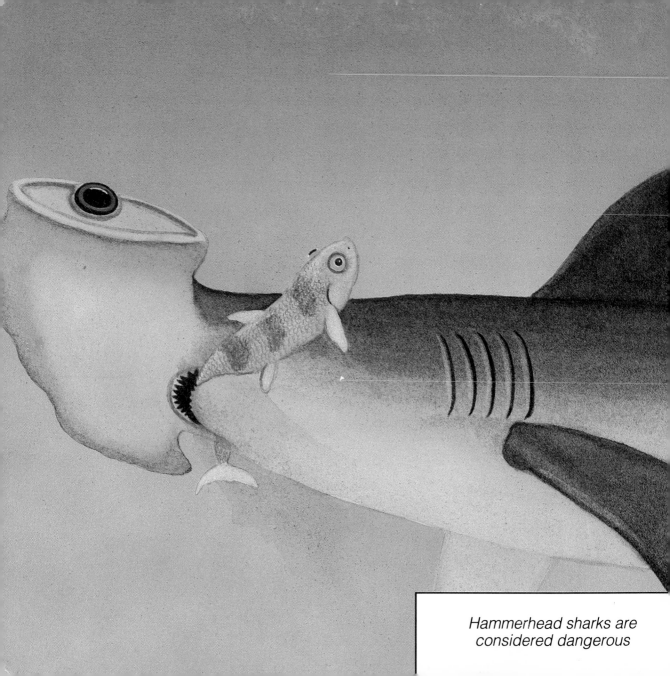

Hammerhead sharks are considered dangerous

Great Hammerhead sharks are a
greenish color

THEIR EYES

Hammerhead sharks' eyes are located on each end of their heads. Their eyelids slide up from the lower edge of their eyes to cover the sensitive eyeball. Hammerhead sharks' eyes usually close as they bite their **prey**, to protect them. Scientists used to think that sharks had poor eyesight. They now know that sharks can see quite well, even in dim light.

This picture shows the position of a hammerhead's eyes and nostrils

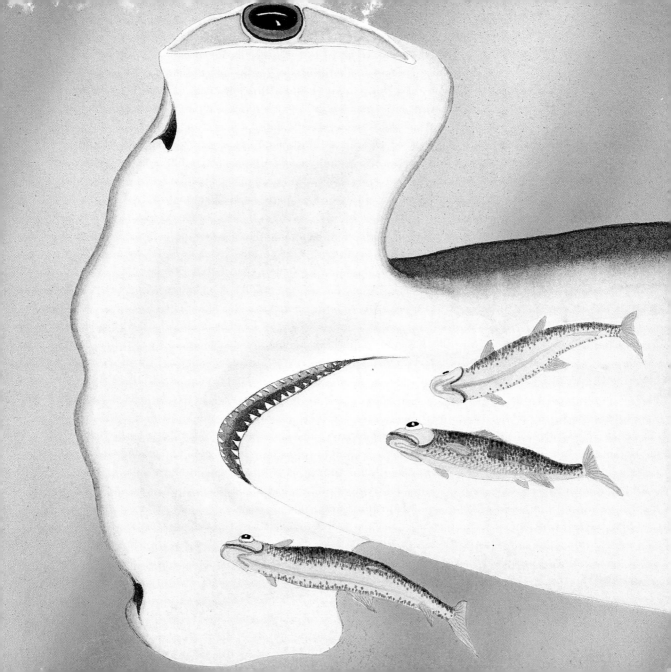

THEIR SENSES

Hammerhead sharks' nostrils are positioned far apart on each end of their hammer-shaped heads, close to their eyes. As the shark breathes, it takes water into its **gills** and nostrils. In the same way that humans find smells in the air when they breathe, sharks find smells in the water. Hammerhead sharks move their heads from side to side as they swim. Scientists think that this movement helps them to pick up smells, because they cover a wider area.

Hammerheads swing their heads from side to side as they swim

SHARK ATTACK!

Most hammerhead sharks are considered dangerous. When people are in trouble and are easy prey, they are often the first sharks to arrive. Hammerhead sharks arrive at the scene of a tragedy in large groups, or **schools**. Great Hammerheads are thought to be man-eaters. Scalloped Hammerheads have been blamed for some attacks on humans, but scientists have found them harmless in captivity.

A school of hammerhead sharks arrive at a shipwreck

AVOIDING SHARK ATTACK

At many beaches in the United States nets are set up to catch sharks who come too close to shore. The nets are placed in quite deep water parallel to the shoreline. If a shark swims into the net, he gets tangled up in it and dies. This is a good way of protecting swimmers, but it is not always so good for other sea life. Sometimes harmless dolphins and seals get caught up in the netting and die.

Hammerhead sharks can get caught in shark nets

FACT FILE

Common Name: Great Hammerhead Shark
Scientific Name: Sphyrna mokarran
Color: Greenish brown
Average Size: Male   – 9 feet, 4 inches
                    Female – 12 feet
Where They Live: Shallow waters around reefs
Danger Level: Dangerous shark

Glossary

gills (GILLS) — parts of a fish's body that take oxygen from the the water for it to breathe

prey (PREY) — an animal that is hunted for food

reefs (REEFS) — chains of rocks or sand close to the surface of the ocean

schools (SCHOOLS) — large groups of sharks, or fish

species (SPE cies) — a scientific term meaning kind or type

INDEX